THE C▚▚▚▚AY
RAIL▚▚▚Y

Tim Bryan

SHIRE PUBLICATIONS

Published in Great Britain in 2013 by Shire Publications Ltd, Midland House, West Way, Botley, Oxford OX2 0PH, United Kingdom.

43-01 21st Street, Suite 220B, Long Island City, NY 11101, USA.

E-mail: shire@shirebooks.co.uk   www.shirebooks.co.uk

© 2013 Tim Bryan.

Every attempt has been made by the Publishers to secure the appropriate permissions for materials reproduced in this book. If there has been any oversight we will be happy to rectify the situation and a written submission should be made to the Publishers.

A CIP catalogue record for this book is available from the British Library.

Shire Library no. 756.   ISBN-13: 978 0 74781 254 8

Tim Bryan has asserted his right under the Copyright, Designs and Patents Act, 1988, to be identified as the author of this book.

Designed by Tony Truscott Designs, Sussex, UK and typeset in Perpetua and Gill Sans.

Printed in China through Worldprint Ltd.

13 14 15 16 17   10 9 8 7 6 5 4 3 2 1

COVER IMAGE
Cattle being loaded at a rural station on the LMS in the 1930s. Stations in country areas were particularly busy on market days and before and after agricultural shows and fairs held each summer.

TITLE PAGE IMAGE
The crew of ex-London & South Western Railway '02' Class 0-4-4 are deep in conversation at Ventnor station on the Isle of Wight in July 1965.

CONTENTS PAGE IMAGE
This Edwardian postcard shows staff and passengers in front of a Southwold Railway train. The railway opened in 1879 and closed in 1929.

ACKNOWLEDGEMENTS
I am grateful to all those who helped locate images for this book, in particular Elaine Arthurs, Collections Officer at STEAM: Museum of the Great Western Railway and Laurence Waters of the Great Western Trust Didcot. Thanks are also due to Steve Andrews of Classic Traction (www.classicsteamphotographics.weebly.com), Owen Bushell of the M&GN Joint Railway Society (www.mandgn.co.uk) Ron Fisher, David Hey, Phil Kelley, Keith Long and Phil Spencer.

As always, thanks are due to my wife Ann who put up with my absences while I wrote the book, and also checked and edited the text.

Illustrations were supplied from the following sources:

David Christie, title page; Classic Traction, page 60; Great Western Trust, pages 4, 5, 33 (top) and 41; Ron Fisher pages 37 and 58; Ironbridge Gorge Museum Trust, page 19; Philip Kelley, page 46 (both); Barry Lewis, pages 6 and 45; Keith Long, pages 9, 13, 19, 34, 47 and 51; Mary Evans Picture Library, front cover; Midland & Great Northern Joint Railway Society Archive, pages 23, 24 and 50; Terry Pinnegar, page 47: Science & Society Picture Library, pages 20, 30, 37, 39 (top) and 40; Phil Spencer, page 9; William Wright, page 57; Author's Collection, pages 12 (top), 14 (top), 32 (bottom), 36 (bottom), 39 (both), 56 (both), 57, 58, 59 and 60.

All other photographs are from the collection of STEAM: Museum of the GWR Swindon (www.steampicturelibrary.com).

Shire Publications is supporting the Woodland Trust, the UK's leading woodland conservation charity, by funding the dedication of trees.

CONTENTS

INTRODUCTION

WHILE THE COMING OF THE RAILWAYS to Britain's towns and cities in the nineteenth century transformed their fortunes and gave urban dwellers new opportunities to travel across Britain, the effect on the largely rural population of the country was arguably far greater. The new main lines such as the Great Western Railway and London & Birmingham were designed to link major cities, and so, while they ran through the countryside, they were not truly country railways; initially at least, railway companies were preoccupied with building inter-city routes and so it was the network of smaller cross-country and branch lines that followed which opened up large tracts of previously remote countryside, providing new markets for agricultural produce, and also ending the isolation of many rural communities.

Such was the pace of development during the Railway Mania period that by the end of the nineteenth century there were few areas of Britain not served by railway. Smaller independent companies such as the Midland & South Western Junction Railway, or the Somerset & Dorset, operated relatively long routes, often serving sparsely populated regions; larger operations too, such

All the railway companies used images of the places and countryside they served to promote their lines. This leaflet issued by the GWR celebrated places of interest around Stratford-upon-Avon in Warwickshire.

4

as the Caledonian or Great Eastern, also operated rural services, providing a vital link for rural communities. Large areas of Wales were also served by railways, including the Cambrian, whose network included many miles of single-track line across remote parts of the principality.

MARKET DAY

CHEAP DAY TICKETS
TO
HEREFORD
EACH WEDNESDAY
FROM THIS STATION

This poster image of Hereford is highly stylised but illustrates how railways played a key role in the life of the countryside, linking smaller communities to larger market towns.

A Southern Railway 'H' Class 0-4-4 waits at Paddock Wood station on 27 October 1960 before taking a branch train to Hawkhurst.

No machine tools are in evidence in this view of the excavations for Chedworth Tunnel on the Swindon & Cheltenham Extension Railway, later part of the MSWJR.

For many railway enthusiasts, however, the country railway is typified by the shorter but nonetheless important branch line. Many of these railways began life as independent companies promoted by local people wishing to ensure their community was linked to the main line, but inevitably they

LNWR 2-4-0
No. 2157 *Unicorn*
waits at
Whitchurch with
a goods train.
The cattle wagons
show evidence
of having been
disinfected with
liberal amounts
of lime.

were often taken over by large railways such as the Great Western, but remained an important part of the districts and communities they served.

Many rural lines proved uneconomic from their earliest days, but, despite some closures in the years before the Second World War, the network remained largely untouched until 1948, despite the increasing importance of road competition, which had reduced already slender receipts on many lines. It was not until after nationalisation and later the publication of

The Somerset
& Dorset is
remembered
as one of
Britain's best-loved
cross-country
lines. In this image
a 7F 2-8-0 is seen
at Radstock in
May 1958.

This view of Stow-on-the-Wold station on the Banbury and Cheltenham route shows at least five staff, and the stationmaster's wife peeping out of the door of the station building.

the Beeching Report in the 1960s that wholesale closure of rural lines took place, to the dismay of local communities.

While well-known lines were axed, the closure programme also marked the blossoming of the fledgling railway preservation movement as enthusiasts banded together to buy and rescue railways. Today the heritage railway movement includes many railways saved during that period and they now enable people to experience something of the atmosphere of a country railway in the golden age of steam. On the privatised railway network too, a number of branch and cross-country routes such as the West Highland Railway and seaside branch lines in the West Country,

An ex-GWR diesel railcar pauses at Chipping Norton station in British Railways days. Passengers are scarce in this view.

Ex-Southern
Railway M7 class
0-4-4T No. 53
arrives at
Corfe Castle
station on the
Swanage Railway
heritage line in
September 2012.

survive away from the main lines, and as the popularity of rail travel
continues to grow, more reopenings are likely in the future, ensuring
that the country railway will survive, although on a rather smaller scale
than in the past.

The branch line
survives in many
places in Britain.
A two-car
'sprinter' runs
along the coast
at Carbis Bay
in Cornwall.

BUILDING COUNTRY RAILWAYS

IN THE YEARS following the opening of the Liverpool & Manchester Railway in 1830 a number of substantial main-line railways were promoted or opened. Lines such as the London & Birmingham, Great Western and London & Southampton were built across great tracts of countryside and by 1843 there were more than 2,000 miles of railway in operation. This modest total was eclipsed in what became known as the Railway Mania; in 1845 and the two years that followed it Parliament authorised more than 650 schemes, which included more than 9,000 miles of track. Inevitably, this speculative bubble burst, leaving many investors out of pocket and schemes unfinished or delayed. By 1860, however, the main-line network was to a large extent complete and the process of linking smaller towns and villages not already on main-line railways was well under way.

The first main lines were built and promoted to link large centres of population and industry and, although much was made of the benefits likely to be gained by the population of the countryside crossed by these new lines, initially at least railway companies did little to generate much business from intermediate stations. The direct nature of many of the new main lines also meant that they bypassed some larger towns that by their population or industry might have expected to be on the railway network. This group included large settlements such as Bedford, Bradford, Halifax, Oxford and Worcester; some towns, anxious not to be left behind, were early pioneers in promoting branches to link them with newly built trunk lines. These short lines to locations such as Oxford, Windsor and Maidstone, built in the 1840s, were in the minority and the process of building branch and minor lines to provide links between trunk lines continued for a further half a century.

Although companies such as the Great Western and North Eastern did finance and build their own branch lines, many of the larger railways were heavily committed to completing and maintaining their main-line systems. As a consequence a large number of cross-country and branch lines were promoted by local landowners or businessmen who, having failed to persuade an existing railway to build the line, instead encouraged people living in

Opposite:
Navvies at
work excavating
a cutting.

Surveying the railway, as seen in F. S. Williams's 1852 book *Our Iron Roads*.

An early view of Dowles Bridge over the River Severn on the Tenbury & Bewdley Railway.

the countryside around a proposed railway to invest in a new company established for the purpose. Before construction could begin, there was much to be done: public meetings were held to drum up support for a new line and to encourage local people to invest. To enable plans for a new line to be put before Parliament for approval, and for a prospectus to be issued,

a survey of the proposed route needed to be completed. This was not always a straightforward exercise, since many people were opposed to railway development; railway engineers and surveyors had to walk the route of the whole line in all weathers, and in the process often faced obstruction, threats and even physical violence from landowners, farmers and others who tried to prevent them from completing their work.

With the survey of the route complete, the engineer would draw up plans that were submitted both to Parliament and to local authorities. As well as the plan of the line, a book of reference listing landowners and occupiers of properties affected by the new railway was also produced. What then followed was a period of what was called by the writer F. S. Williams, 'fighting for the act': a process that took place both in a Parliamentary committee, where formal objections to the building of a railway were debated, and outside Westminster, where the railway negotiated with landowners over compensation arrangements for loss of land or amenities. In many cases the demands made by those across whose land railways were to run were high; claims were made not only for loss of agricultural land, but also loss of crops and disturbance to livestock.

Many landowners made outrageous demands in the hope that the railway would settle with them to ensure that the bill would succeed; many

The twenty-one-arch concrete Glenfinnan Viaduct on the West Highland Railway, was completed in October 1898; this graceful structure cost £18,904. It is now recognised around the world as the viaduct used by the Hogwarts Express in the Harry Potter films.

Woburn station, as seen in 1852, shortly after it opened. It was one of four 'cottage' style buildings unique to the Marston Vale Line.

Moreton-in-Marsh station was also built in a rustic style. This evocative view from the 1930s also shows an Austin Seven car parked outside.

ultimately accepted rather less than first requested, but in some cases railway companies did 'buy off' potentially troublesome opponents, paying large sums of money for relatively small pieces of land, essentially to purchase consent for the scheme. Where railways crossed country estates they often encountered particular difficulties. Railways were often forced to pay compensation to aristocratic landowners and to incur additional expense by hiding the railway from view in tunnels or cuttings, or screening views of the line by the planting of trees. The landed gentry were not beyond demanding excessive amounts of compensation either, and often extracted further concessions, such as the provision of private stations, often built on a grand scale.

Once opposition to the scheme had been overcome, and landowners along the route of the railway placated or bought off, if the Act of Parliament for the railway was passed, the difficult task of raising the necessary capital to build the line was undertaken. Local people were encouraged to invest in their railway, with wildly optimistic claims being made about the viability of the proposed railway in order to secure funding, although in many cases the hoped-for profits never materialised. While local investors and supporters of the railway were enthusiastic about its potential success, when construction finally began they were often less keen on the impact made by the arrival of large numbers of navvies to the area, employed to construct the line.

No health and safety precautions in sight as workmen stand on the top of the partially completed viaduct at High Wycombe.

The commencement of a new railway was usually marked by a ceremony to 'cut the first sod', attended by directors, shareholders, local dignitaries and navvies dressed in their 'Sunday best'. The first sod was normally cut by a ceremonial spade; after this the assembled group marked the occasion with a lunch or dinner. Much has been written about the navvies: their bad reputation often preceded them and the effects of their stay in a quiet country village during the building of a branch or minor line cannot be underestimated. Drunkenness and violence were common but it was lack of accommodation that caused the most difficulty. On the West Highland Railway the remoteness of the area through which the railway was being built made matters worse. Over five thousand navvies were employed to build the railway, and were housed in isolated camps along the route of the line. In an effort to reduce drunkenness, the company paid part of their wages in the form of food that they could cook for themselves, and the services of church missionaries and Temperance Union representatives were required. Conditions in the camps provided for navvies were often squalid and the antagonism between them and local residents did not help.

The navvies were normally employed by railway contractors who built either the whole line or sections, depending on its length. The time taken to

A view of Lower Dowdeswell viaduct on the Banbury & Cheltenham Direct Railway after widening in 1899.

The scene at Toddington in Gloucestershire showing the temporary accommodation provided for navvies building the Honeybourne line for the GWR in 1904.

complete the railway depended heavily on the terrain to be crossed and the number of physical barriers such as rivers and hills on the route. In addition to these difficulties, railway contractors also had to contend with the weather. In the case of the Keighley & Worth Valley Railway in Yorkshire, for example, progress on the construction was slow; severe storms in the winter of 1866 led to sections of the line being washed away, putting back the opening of the railway until the following year. These difficulties notwithstanding,

The elaborate decorations provided on the cast-iron columns supporting the canopy at Great Malvern station.

construction normally proceeded apace and the final stage in the process was the visit of the Railway Inspector, who ensured that the new line was safe.

In a world where innovation and new developments are perhaps more commonplace than in the past, it is hard to imagine the excitement felt by residents of country towns and villages about the opening of their branch line. After the trials and tribulations of its construction, the new railway promised much and as a result the local population celebrated its opening in style, with a special first train carrying dignitaries and directors cheered off on an inaugural trip from one end of the line to the other. The day was rounded off – as it often was in the Victorian era – by a feast, with drinking and festivities such as dancing and sport.

Once the festivities were over, the railway soon became part of the landscape; within a few years the scars made by the construction work had healed as trees and vegetation grew. By the 1880s many smaller towns and villages were finally connected to the railway network and were provided

Staff, dignitaries and public await the arrival of the first train at the opening of the Yealmpton branch on 15 January 1898.

with facilities of the highest quality. Many branch and minor lines were built to main-line standards and thus provided with grand and over-large stations that would never justify the levels of business they would ultimately generate. This was undoubtedly prompted largely by over-ambitious estimates of the revenues likely to be achieved, but these over-engineered structures also left railways with ongoing maintenance costs that their revenues could not cover. The independent companies promoting railways had also underestimated the costs of engineering work required to complete even the most straightforward lines; final costs were much higher than anticipated, leaving them with considerable debt at the outset. It was only when the Light Railways Act was passed in 1896 that cheaper, less heavily engineered lines were built, with lower running costs, although even these routes were built too late since road competition would soon begin to impact on railway revenues.

The consequence of much misplaced optimism and, in some cases, reckless spending, was that within a few years many independent branches and cross-country routes were struggling to generate enough revenue to cover running costs and service debt and depreciation costs. The goods and passenger traffic receipts predicted by promoters rarely materialised; with little money to invest, lines became run-down. As a result, many companies had little choice but to amalgamate with bigger concerns, making little, if any profit for their shareholders, but ultimately ensuring the longer-term survival of the railway. In many cases, railways such as the GWR, when taking over small independent companies also had to spend considerable sums, upgrading permanent way and replacing non-standard locomotives and rolling stock to bring the services up to scratch. Some independent companies struggled on, but even they were eventually swallowed up in 1923 when the 'Big Four' companies were created.

Timber viaducts were a distinctive feature of railways designed by I. K. Brunel in the Devon and Cornwall countryside. This structure west of St Austell was eventually replaced by a masonry viaduct in 1898.

ACROSS THE
COUNTRYSIDE

IN CONTRAST to the shorter branch lines that linked main-line junctions with rural communities, longer cross-country lines ran across the countryside, often through sparsely populated areas of Britain. Whilst main lines linked large centres of population, the minor routes opened up remoter areas, providing new markets for agricultural produce and minerals traffic such as stone and slate and also ending years of isolation for many rural communities.

The Central Wales line, running from Shrewsbury to Swansea, was built by the London & North Western Railway to penetrate deep into the heart of GWR territory. The railway survives today; at well over 90 miles long, the route is rather too long to be described as a branch line, but with over half of its route being single track it is hardly a main line either.

The construction of the Central Wales Railway took almost twenty-eight years, the line being the combination of five companies that together enabled through trains to run from Shrewsbury to South Wales. Although eventually part of the LNWR, the route incorporated the Llanelly Railway, the Vale of Towy Railway, the Knighton Railway, and the Central Wales and Central Wales Extension Railway. Built through the heart of mid-Wales, the line passes through some spectacular scenery, and features fearsome gradients and a number of impressive viaducts and tunnels.

One of the best-known cross-country routes was the Somerset & Dorset, which until its closure in 1966 was one of the most distinctive and well-loved lines on the British Railways network. Although it always struggled to make any money, and was an independent operation for only a short time, it maintained its own distinctive identity right up to the day it closed. The Somerset & Dorset Company was created from the amalgamation of the Somerset Central Railway (whose lines linked Glastonbury, Wells, Highbridge and Burnham-on-Sea) with the Dorset Central, whose route ran from Wimborne to Blandford and eventually north to Templecombe.

The amalgamated company struggled to survive, pinning its hopes on the construction of a new 26-mile line over the Mendip Hills from Evercreech to Bath, which cost over £400,000 in 1872. The route was

Opposite:
Detail of a 1930s poster of Monsal Dale Viaduct in Derbyshire, based on a painting by the artist Norman Wilkinson for the London Midland & Scottish Railway.

characterised by steep inclines, many built to a 1-in-50 gradient, four substantial tunnels and seven viaducts. Built in only two years, the Bath Extension ran through the North Somerset coalfield, and it was hoped that the railway could generate substantial income from serving coalmines at locations such as Radstock. At the Bath end of the line Somerset & Dorset trains joined the Midland Railway at a junction west of the city and ran into a grand new terminus at Green Park.

Continuing financial difficulties meant that the route was leased by the Midland and London & South Western railways in 1876. Despite the operating difficulties presented by the route, it became an important link between the Midlands, the North of England and the south coast, for both freight and passenger services, and its cross-country route also ensured that it was an important artery for military traffic in the Second World War. After the war it underwent a renaissance especially in the holiday season, when many important north–south expresses ran over the line – including the famous Manchester–Bournemouth 'Pines Express'. This traffic had diminished by the early 1960s and the line was closed in 1966.

Two other cross-country routes that linked the south coast with the Midlands and the North were the Didcot, Newbury & Southampton Railway and the Midland & South Western Junction Railway, both taken over by

An early view of the Somerset & Dorset Railway, showing 4-4-0 No. 15, one of a number built by the Midland Railway at Derby in 1891.

the Great Western at grouping in 1923. The DNS opened from Didcot to Newbury in 1882 and through to Winchester three years later. It had been intended that the railway would continue to Southampton, but lack of finance meant that trains had to use LSWR tracks to reach the port instead. The railway was built across a very sparsely populated area, climbing up from the Thames Valley on to chalk uplands; traffic was always light on the route, and for most of its life the railway had only four or five stopping trains each way on weekdays. It became of great importance only during the Second World War, when it was a vital link between armaments factories in the Midlands and south coast ports used for the D-Day landings in 1944.

Midland &Great Northern 4-4-0 No. 24 'A Class' approaching Weybourne with a down express, *c.* 1900.

Further west, the Midland & South Western Junction Railway, also part of the GWR after 1923, performed a similar role in the Second World War. Whereas the DNS crossed rural Berkshire and Hampshire, the MSWJR route ran from Cheltenham in the north across the Cotswolds to Swindon, crossing the GWR main line there before continuing south over the Marlborough Downs through Savernake Forest and on to Andover. The MSWJR was the amalgamation of two companies: the Swindon & Cheltenham Extension Railway and the Swindon, Marlborough & Andover Railway.

Opened throughout in 1891, it was hoped that profitable passenger and goods services could be run from the North of England to the south coast,

but this business failed to develop sufficiently, and the largely agricultural country served by the railway did not generate enough local traffic either. When absorbed by the GWR in 1923, its finances had recovered somewhat but it was never a profitable operation, like the DNS proving important only during both World Wars, both for through traffic and for the running of trains serving military bases and camps on Salisbury Plain.

Many of the cross-country railways remained proudly independent and none more so than the Midland & Great Northern Railway, an operation that came to encompass a network of over 180 miles of railway in East Anglia. One railway writer has described it as a 'classic rural railway', with much of its route being single track, serving largely remote local communities in Norfolk as well as busier holiday resorts on the coast. The MGNR was created not as one company but as the result of the amalgamation of a number of smaller lines built from the 1850s onwards, which eventually joined together as the Eastern & Midlands Railway.

The company crest of the Midland & Great Northern Railway.

This operation was jointly taken over by the Midland and Great Northern companies in 1893 to create a railway that linked Spalding and Peterborough in the west with King's Lynn, Cromer, Lowestoft and Yarmouth on the Norfolk coast. At the centre of the M&GN network was Melton Constable, a sleepy village with a population of only 118 in 1881; within years it was transformed with the construction of the company's locomotive works, complete with houses and a railway institute; it was nicknamed

An atmospheric amateur picture of GWR 4-4-0 No. 3289 hauling the 1.35pm Cheltenham express on the MSWJR line near Chedworth on 29 June 1932.

locally the 'Crewe of North Norfolk'. The rural nature of the area served by the railway and the rich soil of East Anglia meant that its freight business included much agricultural produce, including apples, pears, plums, gooseberries and other soft fruit from Wisbech, potatoes from the Spalding area, and mustard and starch from the Colman Company in Norwich. On the coast, the railway was also able to generate considerable income from fish traffic. The railway also carried thousands of holidaymakers from the industrial heartlands of the Midlands, the North and Scotland to resorts such as Cromer and Great Yarmouth.

In contrast to the countryside crossed by the rambling MGNR network in Norfolk was the bleak and unforgiving Pennine landscape encountered by travellers on the railway linking Tebay in Westmorland (now Cumbria) to Bishop Auckland in County Durham. The South Durham & Lancashire Railway, also known as the Stainmore Railway (opened in 1862), had

Much of the extensive Cambrian Railways network ran through rural Wales, with lines running along the coasts of Cardiganshire and Merionethshire. This view of 4-4-0 No. 60 and crew was taken at Pwllheli.

On many cross-country routes over hilly terrain, snow was a hazard in winter. Many railways provided snow ploughs, either as separate wagons coupled in front of engines, or bolted to the front of engines, as was the case in this GWR picture of a Dean Goods engine, taken in 1904.

connections with other railways, enabling trains to run through from the Lake District in the west to Darlington in the east. As well as providing a through route between the East- and West-coast main lines to Scotland, and a connection between LMS and LNER networks, it was also an important freight line, linking the collieries and steel works of Northumberland to the shipyards of Barrow and the iron ore mines of Cumberland.

The route crossed some challenging terrain, both for those who originally built the line, and for those who subsequently operated it; the railway climbed some formidable gradients across the moors from Kirkby Stephen to Stainmore Summit (1,370 feet above sea level) and crossed a number of Pennine valleys on spectacular wrought-iron viaducts. Trains were often double-headed or required the assistance of banking engines; in winter the route was often closed by snow.

LAKE DISTRICT EXPRESS. F.R.

Another cross-country line traversing spectacular scenery is the West Highland route, which, unlike the Stainmore line, remains open. The line is seen by many as one of the greatest railway journeys in the world and although, after road improvements completed in the 1980s, the trip from Glasgow to Mallaig can now be accomplished more quickly by car, thousands still use the line, many travelling on steam-hauled services in the summer months. The West Highland Railway opened in two stages: the section from Glasgow to Fort William was completed in 1894, with a further extension to Mallaig not finished until 1901.

The route passed through miles of uninhabited mountains with few settlements of any real importance and doubts were voiced as to whether the railway would ever make any money. The completion of the line did, however, end the isolation of the Western Highlands and Islands, which had been previously accessible only by sea or a long carriage journey. In later years, trains carried thousands of tourists to Fort William and beyond, and also enabled fish to be quickly moved from ports such as Mallaig to Scottish cities and further afield. Both the line to Fort William and the extension to Mallaig beyond crossed some difficult terrain, with mountain, moor and valley presenting formidable problems for the engineers and navvies who built the railway. Since they were high in the mountains, stations were built in the Swiss style, many being island platform structures. Attention was given to the welfare of sheep, deer and other

A Highland Railway Perth–Inverness express hauled by No. 44 *Blair Castle* around 1910.

Opposite, bottom: The Furness Railway began life as a route serving the mines, shipyards and industry of Barrow-in-Furness, but expanded dramatically in the late nineteenth century, developing its network to bring holidaymakers from northern towns into the Lake District.

Above: The Leek & Manifold Light Railway was opened in 1904 and eventually closed in 1934. The Staffordshire narrow-gauge line was taken over by the LMS at grouping in 1923.

Right: A selection of GWR luggage labels.

livestock, an important part of the economy of the Highlands; the West Highland company provided special high fencing and more than two hundred 'creeps' for livestock to cross the line.

There were also a number of longer narrow-gauge and light railways with cross-country routes that were more than just branch lines. The Welsh Highland Railway, with a 22-mile route that crossed the mountains of Snowdonia from Caernarfon to Porthmadog, had a complicated history, and origins in the slate industry of North Wales. Opened throughout as a light railway in 1923, the line struggled to survive from its inception and, despite being leased by the Festiniog Railway in 1934,

the revenue from passengers and goods was poor and it closed in 1937. It was reopened as a heritage railway in 2011 after years of restoration work by volunteers.

A sepia postcard view of Blackmore Gate station on the Lynton & Barnstaple Railway.

The Lynton & Barnstaple Railway was also a narrow-gauge concern, which opened in 1898. The line had been promoted because the twin villages of Lynton and Lynmouth on the North Devon coast were almost 20 miles from the nearest main-line station and were accessible only by an uncomfortable carriage ride from Barnstaple. The 1-foot 11-inch gauge railway constructed over Exmoor cost far more than expected because of the terrain, and the 19¼ mile line that was built across the moors included many cuttings, embankments and bridges. Despite the expectations of the promoters, the line was never very profitable and was taken over by the Southern Railway in 1923.

By the end of the nineteenth century, many towns and villages had been connected to the railway system through branch or cross-country routes, but there were still some places without a rail link. The Light Railways Act of 1896 enabled cheaper and less heavily engineered railways to be constructed, such as the Weston, Clevedon & Portishead, Kent & East Sussex, and Leek & Manifold railways. Despite having very basic facilities and relatively low running costs, many light railways struggled against road competition and few survived after 1930.

BRANCH LINES

W HILST MANY enthusiasts have great affection for minor cross-country routes now long gone, such as the Somerset & Dorset, those with more than a little nostalgia for old railways remember most fondly the rural branch line. Although many branch lines were built to serve all types of communities and also linked holiday resorts, harbours, mines, quarries and other locations, it is the image of a sleepy single-track railway running through fields and countryside that still resonates with many. A typical trip on one of these lines would usually begin at a larger junction station, where the branch train would leave from a bay platform after connecting with a main-line train. Most services would consist of a locomotive and one or two carriages, with both engine and rolling stock often being rather elderly. The train would wind its way along the branch, pausing at wayside stations or halts before ending its journey at a terminus where the usually modest numbers of passengers would leave the train to be greeted by station staff who often knew them by name.

Nowhere was the country branch line better represented than on the Great Western Railway. It was by no means the only railway to have such routes, but many well-known branch lines in the West of England were under GWR control. Just north of Swindon, Kemble served as the junction for two branch lines. The first, to the market town of Cirencester, was opened as early as 1841 by the Cheltenham & Great Western Union Railway and had only two intermediate stations on the 5-mile line. The Brunel-designed station building in Cirencester still survives in a town centre car park. To the west of Kemble another branch ran across open countryside to the Gloucestershire market town of Tetbury. The 7¼-mile line had three small intermediate stations and was opened in 1889, following the failure of a more ambitious scheme to build a railway from Stroud to Malmesbury. Goods traffic was modest, despite being bolstered by the opening of a cattle market close to the Tetbury terminus; passenger numbers were never large. In 1959, four-wheeled diesel railcars were introduced on the branch to boost traffic, but despite an increase in business the line was one of those axed in the Beeching Report and it closed in 1964.

Opposite:
The wagon being loaded onto a LMS wagon was part of a farm removal undertaken by the railway in 1937. Furniture, livestock and equipment were all shifted as part of this service.

The scene at Hemyock in Devon. The small cabin next to the station building contained the lever frame controlling the points and signals. Beyond the station can be seen the creamery that provided much of the income for the branch during its life.

Opposite, top left: A view of the Wye Valley line, showing the railway at Symonds Yat.

Below: Brunel's station at Cirencester, on the branch from Kemble, still survives – although much neglected and in the middle of a car park.

A number of the best-known Great Western branches were located in Devon and Cornwall. The Hemyock branch line began life as the independent Culm Valley Railway linking the Devon town of Tiverton with the small village of Hemyock. The railway was promoted by local interests and built relatively cheaply, its 7¼-mile route following the course of the river Culm, with a number of intermediate stations. The railway was taken over by the GWR in 1880, and while passenger revenues were modest, with only four trains a day being run, goods receipts were better, boosted by the opening in 1886 of a dairy at Hemyock that continued to provide traffic for the line right up to its complete closure in 1975.

Away from the bucolic delights of the West of England, the Midland Railway built and operated a number of branch lines in territory seen by the Great Northern and LNWR as rightfully theirs. In Derbyshire the Wirksworth line was a good example of this practice, opened for traffic in 1867. Passenger traffic on the branch was never substantial, but freight business in the form of limestone was far more important, as was the movement of milk, at

SMILING SOMERSET

Left: Away from the coast, railways also promoted country areas as places to stay and walk, especially in the 1920s and 1930s, as a way of generating more traffic over rural lines.

Below: A double-headed train on the ex-Midland Railway Keighley & Worth Valley branch, now operating as a heritage railway.

one time amounting to almost 800,000 gallons each day. The Derbyshire spa town of Buxton was also the scene of railway competition, being served by both Midland and LNWR lines until the 1960s. The Midland branch ran from Millers Dale on the clumsily named Manchester, Buxton, Matlock & Midlands Railway, by which the MR hoped to link Birmingham, Derby and Manchester.

Further north, another branch built to serve the textile trade eventually became one of the best-known preserved railways in Britain. The MR route from Leeds to Skipton already ran through the town of Keighley and so it was decided that a new branch line would run from Oxenhope through Haworth terminating at the existing station in Keighley. With the support of the Midland Railway, the directors of the new line – to be called the Keighley & Worth Valley Railway – obtained an Act of Parliament and raised the £36,000 needed to build the line. When the railway first opened it was

Southern Region 'H' class 0-4-4T No. 31551 waits to depart from Paddock Wood for Hawkhurst on a rainy day in October 1960. The branch line closed the following year.

operated by the Midland in return for 50 per cent of the profits, but by 1881 had been completely absorbed by the Midland, which continued to operate the branch until it became part of the LMS in 1923.

In contrast to other 'Big Four' companies, the branch railways operated by the Southern in its rural areas varied enormously. After grouping, the company spent considerable sums modernising and electrifying its main lines and suburban routes, but little investment was made on rural lines and they remained the preserve of elderly locomotives and rolling stock. This meant that there was no such thing as a 'typical' SR branch line. The geographical area served by the Southern stretched from the Thames estuary and Kent to the east across a large swathe of southern England, even reaching into Devon and Cornwall. Right across the network, highly individual rural branches were operated by the Southern, each varying according to its history and the landscape it crossed.

One of the oldest branch lines operated by the SR was the line originally built as the Canterbury & Whitstable Railway in Kent. Only 6 miles long, the railway was engineered by George Stephenson, and opened as early as May 1830. The line ran north from Canterbury to Whitstable on the Kent coast and had to overcome some difficult terrain. The tunnel at Tyler Hill was the first ever to be used by passenger services and had both restricted clearances and a 1-in-56 gradient, making it difficult for locomotive crews. As a result, locomotives used on the line were modified with cut-down cab roofs, chimneys and boiler mountings. Passenger services on the branch were withdrawn in 1931, although goods traffic continued to use the line until 1952.

Stroudley 'Terrier' 0-6-0 tank engines such as 'Denmark' were used extensively on branch lines in Sussex as the main-line network in the south-east of England was electrified.

35

As befitted a railway built with a relatively modest budget, the common seal of the Cleobury Mortimer & Ditton Priors Railway was also modest, with none of the decoration common on seals of earlier railways.

A more conventional and newer branch line ran from Paddock Wood to Hawkhurst in Kent, operated by the South Eastern & Chatham Railway. The 11½-mile railway ran south from Paddock Wood via the village of Goudhurst to Hawkhurst and was opened in 1892. The line ran across remote hilly Kent countryside in what became known as the 'Garden of England' and the SECR and Southern ran special trains taking workers to help harvest the hops grown in the area. Although there were connections with main-line services at Paddock Wood, the branch was never very busy; the location of stations on the branch was not helpful in attracting business and both Cranbrook and Hawkhurst stations were situated almost 2 miles from the settlements they served.

The Southern acquired the short but picturesque Lyme Regis branch when it absorbed the LSWR in 1923. The 6¾-mile line had been promoted by the Axminster & Lyme Regis Light Railway, but was operated by the LSWR from opening in 1903. Passengers changed at Axminster and took a train down the branch, which wound its way to Lyme, with only one intermediate station, serving the village of Compbyne. Steep gradients and tight curves on the line meant that working the branch was not easy. An attractive station was provided at Lyme Regis, but its location about half a mile from the town – and more importantly 250 feet above the sea – made it less than popular with weary holidaymakers trudging up the hill to catch their train after a day on the beach! The Southern also served resorts on the Devon coast, with branches to both Sidmouth and Exmouth.

While most Cornish branch lines carried thousands of passengers each year, others also generated goods business. The Fowey branch dealt with thousands of tons of china clay each year. This scene was recorded in May 1959.

A motor
charabanc full of
tourists leaving
Windermere
station in 1909 on
a trip to Grasmere
in the Lake
District. Many
country railways
were vital links in
developing the
tourist trade

Visitors of a rather grander kind used the branch line from Aberdeen to Ballater. Originally built by the Deeside Railway, the single-track branch opened through to Ballater in 1869 and was subsequently operated by the Great North of Scotland Railway until grouping in 1923. The Deeside line ran through stunning highland scenery, carrying tourists and walkers, but was also the route used by British and foreign royalty and heads of state on their way to visit Queen Victoria at her Balmoral estate. The Queen used the line until just before her death in 1901 and in 1886 a grand royal waiting room was built at Ballater. A paper mill served by the railway also generated goods traffic for the line, but, although the royal family continued to use the branch, it was another casualty of the Beeching Report, closing to passengers in 1966.

The narrow-gauge Campbeltown & Machrihanish, an unusual and long-defunct light railway, carried both coal and passengers, and operated on the west coast of Scotland until the 1930s. The line originally opened in 1877 to serve collieries in and around Campbeltown but was extended between 1904 and 1906 to carry passengers to nearby Machrihanish, extending the branch to just over 6 miles long. As much of the collieries' output was consumed locally, the railway's freight business was seasonal, and so carrying tourists in summer was ideal. In the years before the First World War, by replacing local horse bus services, the railway was very successful, but increased competition from motor-bus operators and industrial unrest in the mines led to the line closing by 1934.

Narrow-gauge and light railway branches were built in some numbers after 1890, linking mines, quarries and other industrial centres, or running passenger services. A number of these still survive as heritage railways; in mid-Wales the 2-foot 6-inch gauge Welshpool & Llanfair Light Railway

opened in 1903 following a public enquiry that had rejected the idea of a standard-gauge branch line. At just over 9 miles long, the short branch included some sharp curves and a 1-in-29 gradient, making it difficult to operate. Worked by the Cambrian and then the GWR, the railway struggled to survive. However, revenue from the movement of cattle and sheep was healthy under the Great Western although passenger receipts were disappointing and services were abandoned in 1931.

LMS 0-6-0
No. 16118
'Strathpeffer'
at the Scottish
station of the
same name in
August 1926.
Its train
contains a rather
motley selection
of carriages.

A rather different narrow-gauge branch was built on the Suxxex coast in 1895 to carry a very specific type of passenger: the golfer. The increasing popularity of the sport in the 1890s had led to a proliferation of new golf clubs, and, with the opening of Rye Golf Club at Camber Sands in 1894, a 3-foot-gauge railway was built to transport golfers from Rye to the links. The line was built by Colonel Stephens and proved a success, especially when the line was extended to Camber Sands, enabling tourists to visit the beach in summer months. Although it was originally operated by a steam locomotive, in 1924 falling revenues, especially in the winter, forced the railway to replace it with a small petrol locomotive, which ran services until the demise of the line in 1939.

A three-car diesel multiple unit heads for Ashley Hill box, on the Severn Beach branch line in April 1978.

A DAY IN THE LIFE

IT HAS BEEN estimated that there were more than five thousand stations serving rural communities at the zenith of railway operation in Great Britain; until road transport began to change the landscape, the country station was an important gateway through which people and goods passed on their way to towns and cities sometimes many miles away. The rural station was a vital link to the outside world, especially in remoter parts of the country and before the rise of radio and television; it was the place where news arrived – through the delivery of mail, newspapers, or (in the early days of railways) telegraph messages. It was also the scene of arrivals and departures in peace and war and stood at the heart of country communities.

The fact that the life of a country station was interwoven into the life of the community it served was reinforced by the fact that many of the staff employed there often lived locally and worked in the same place for many years. Although working for the railway was largely a very secure profession, pay was not high; however, in rural locations staff might be provided with accommodation close to the station, reinforcing the link with the local community. The best-known railwayman was usually the stationmaster, who as David St John Thomas put it, was in country areas a 'local institution' and played an important role in local affairs. The stationmaster might well have already worked his way up the promotion ladder and, if ambitious for better prospects, might not stay for a long time in one station. As the man in charge, the stationmaster had, as another writer noted, 'to know everything about everybody and to instruct everybody about everything'. In a smaller rural station, he would have had a staff of between six and twenty, depending on the level of traffic, and it was his responsibility to ensure that the station was well run, clean and efficient, and that the men under him performed their duties to the highest standard. The stationmaster also dealt with the voluminous bureaucracy generated by the operation of even the smallest station: accounts, accident reports, changes to fares and goods rates, publicity and advertising, and canvassing of local businesses for trade were all his responsibility. Most stationmasters tried to meet all trains, too, ensuring

Opposite: LMS Goods staff make a delivery to a farm in 1935. All the 'Big Four' companies ran country motor lorry services in the interwar years, replacing the older and slower horse-drawn delivery wagons.

The scene at Bodmin Road (now Bodmin Parkway), c. 1895. Most stations with the word 'road' in the title were usually some miles from the town or village they served, and this was the case with Bodmin. The stationmaster is probably the man with the top hat in the centre of the picture.

Right: Part of a series of front covers celebrating the work of Western Region staff including porters and ticket collectors.

Vol.10 No.7 July 1959

British Railways Magazine 3d

Western Region

PRIDE IN THE JOB

Below: Shunting cattle wagons in the goods yard at Kingsbridge in Devon in 1946.

Opposite page, lower images: GWR labels for loads that needed handling with some care.

that they were a familiar face to passengers using the station.

For most travellers, it was probably a rather more humble porter who greeted most users of country trains, and, while he undoubtedly had as many tasks to complete as the stationmaster, most of these required more demanding physical work. In rural locations porters normally had a varied role: opening and closing the station each day; keeping ticket offices, waiting rooms and passenger toilets clean; selling tickets; dealing with parcels; maintaining gas and oil lamps; and tending coal fires in winter months. It was also the job of the porter to wind and maintain the station clock, and ensure that it showed the correct time; on the GWR a telegraph message was transmitted to all stations every week to allow clocks to be regulated. With more time between train services at country stations, porters and other staff were also able to spend time tending station gardens. Bloxham, on the Banbury & Cheltenham Railway, was famous for its extensive gardens. They included lawns, roses and rockeries, regularly winning competitions held with other stations on the GWR.

At smaller stations porters also assisted goods department staff. Before the onset of road competition, the goods yard at a country station would comprise sidings serving a goods shed, coal yard and livestock pens. On branch lines and quieter cross-country routes, a 'pick-up' goods would normally call each day, dropping off and collecting wagonloads of freight for the station; the shunting of these wagons would be done either by the

The rather ramshackle coal merchant's office at Hook in Hampshire, with the coal yard to the right.

train engine or by horse power, since on many railways, until the 1930s, the delivery and collection of goods was still done using horse-drawn wagons. Goods were unloaded at the shed, checked and then reloaded on to delivery carts or motor lorries. Between the two world wars, the 'Big Four' railways operated 'Country Lorry' services designed to compete with independent hauliers, delivering goods brought to railhead stations by train.

Some stations also catered for special traffic, depending on the location and season; normally quiet branch lines would be briefly transformed during the harvest period when lorry loads of produce would be delivered to goods yards for dispatch. In East Anglia, Great Eastern and Midland & Great Northern stations handled thousands of tons of root vegetables and other produce, while in Kent and Worcestershire railways were particularly busy during the fruit-picking season. Other seasonal crops included Cornish broccoli, Kentish hops and sugar beet from East Anglia. Often traffic was so heavy that cattle wagons and other rolling stock were temporarily pressed into service to carry loads quickly to their destinations.

Heavier loads, such as machinery, timber, building materials and manure, were unloaded out in the goods yard, using a yard crane or mechanically operated mobile crane brought in specially; coal was dealt with in separate sidings allocated to local coal merchants, whose staff unloaded their own wagons. In rural areas stations not surprisingly dealt with livestock of all types, including cattle, pigs and sheep; most country stations had a siding serving a set of cattle or sheep pens where animals could be stabled before shipment or after unloading. Naturally traffic was busier around market days and before and after the larger agricultural fairs and shows held in the summer

months. The level of traffic varied tremendously from place to place: GWR records show that in 1926 the station at Aberaeron handled 376 livestock wagons that year, while Abbotsbury dealt with only thirty-four trucks in the same period. Few station staff enjoyed dealing with unpredictable and sometimes belligerent animals and fewer still enjoyed cleaning out and disinfecting the pens afterwards! Great care was also required in the loading and unloading of horses, transported around the countryside for racing or fox-hunting; horse boxes were normally attached to the rear of a passenger service on a branch line, rather than the horses being marshalled into goods trains. On the Lambourn branch in Berkshire, between the two world wars, race-horse traffic was large and regular enough to warrant the running of special trains that included both horse boxes and carriages for stable staff.

Until the 1930s, when larger milk depots and creameries were built to deal with milk from farms and load it into tanker wagons for dispatch, most country stations were responsible for the daily routine of loading fresh milk for movement to London or other large towns and cities. The task of loading full milk churns was not easy for staff since they were heavy and difficult to handle; the scale of the business was huge, however, and by

Below left: A GWR poster illustrating road services offered for the rural community, particularly farmers.

Below right: In the 1920s and 1930s motor manufacturers such as Thornycroft made many vehicles for the delivery and collection of goods from country and town railway stations.

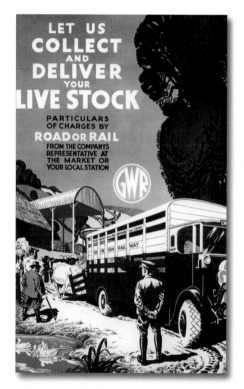

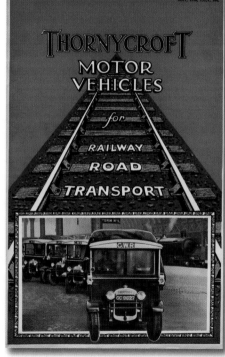

1910, 96 per cent of the milk drunk by Londoners was brought to the capital by rail, much from small, rural stations.

The passenger waiting for a train at a country station might well hear the tinkle of the block bell used to communicate train movements between boxes drifting out of the windows of the signal box at the end of the platform. The life of a signalman on a rural line was very different to that of someone working in a main-line box; trains were fewer in number, leaving more time to keep the box spotlessly clean and for other activities such as maintaining the station allotment – often located next to the signal cabin. At smaller stations signalmen would also issue and check passenger tickets and help out in the parcels office if required.

On many railways, staff began their climb up the promotion ladder by moving from the job of porter to porter signalman, a role that included a good deal of hard manual work such as the cleaning of signal-box windows and linoleum floor and the maintenance of signal lamps in and around the station, a task that entailed climbing up tall signal posts to retrieve lamps. At smaller rural locations signalmen would also be responsible for safely opening and closing level-crossing gates;

The view from the signal box at Beamish Museum's restored Rowley Signal Box. The engine visible through the windows is a Furness Railway 0-4-0 tender engine built in 1863, thought to be the oldest working standard gauge locomotive in Britain.

The Jones family outside the crossing keeper's house at Caedu, including John Evans and his wife Betsy.

A British Railways ganger pictured in 1947 in wintry conditions.

The staff of Cromer Beach Station, 1908; the stationmaster sits in the middle of the first row.

away from the stations, crossing keepers had a rather lonelier job. Before the advent of mechanically operated automatic level crossings, in locations where the landscape did not allow for the provision of a bridge over the line to be possible, railway staff were required to open and close the level-crossing gates manually. Crossing keepers often lived next to the line with their families, but nevertheless worked long shifts in comparison with signal staff.

The country railwaymen who were closest to nature were probably the gangers and platelayers who maintained the permanent way. It was their responsibility to walk their 'length' of track regularly, checking the condition of the rails and sleepers, and also ensuring that

vegetation and undergrowth were cut back to reduce the danger of lineside fires in hot weather. In the case of shorter branch lines, gangers would look after the whole line, rather than individual stretches of track, as was the case on the main line. Permanent way staff also maintained fences and walls so that livestock could not stray on to the line, not only preventing accidents, but also costly insurance claims against railway companies from farmers and landowners. Out in all weathers, winter and summer, track maintenance staff were a tough breed who nevertheless faced the highest risk of being killed or injured on the railway, even on quieter country routes. All the 'Big Four' companies continued to run safety campaigns to try to reduce casualties after the First World War, but accidents were still common even in the 1950s.

This British Railways passenger guard has a flower in his buttonhole. Although the picture was taken in 1965, the uniform had remained largely unchanged for many years.

GWR station staff wait in the goods yard as a train of cattle trucks hauled by a 'Dean Goods' locomotive arrives at Llanaber station in 1934.

DECLINE AND FALL

BY THE EARLY YEARS of the twentieth century there were few places in Britain not directly served by rail or situated relatively close to a railway line. It could be argued that many areas were actually over-provided with rail access, with some towns and villages served by duplicate lines operated by rival companies. By 1914 there were also ominous warning signs that the pre-eminent position of railways was now under threat with the rise of motor buses and cars. Buses were a particular threat, their flexibility and relatively low operating costs making them an attractive proposition; some railways such as the Great Western responded by introducing omnibus services of their own, both as feeders to railway stations and also to compete directly with other operators. Railway companies also began to fight road competition by building more 'halts', small stations in both rural and suburban locations. These were often cheaply built from timber and were unstaffed, keeping running costs for railways low.

An early experiment in railcar operation. This steam railmotor was used by the Taff Vale Railway in South Wales.

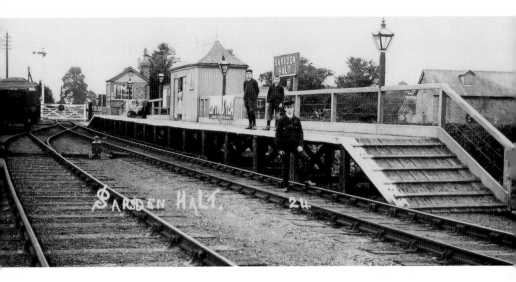

During the First World War, a number of branch lines were closed for the duration, with some even having their rails removed to be melted down for the war effort, something repeated in the Second World War; where branches and minor lines were situated close to military installations and training camps, such as on Salisbury Plain, they played a vital role in the war effort, as did those with stations serving military hospitals, at Netley near Southampton, for example. A number of the branch lines that were closed during the First World War were abandoned completely after it, and others did not reopen immediately. The difficult economic conditions endured by railways in the years after 1918 meant that the management of the 'Big Four' companies created in 1923 needed to reduce costs in order to survive. As early as 1926 the GWR had commissioned a report on its branch lines, to ascertain how many were uneconomic and to look at ways in which costs could be reduced, such as replacing services with motor buses, substituting railmotors for steam locomotives and reducing the number of staff employed at stations. The company also contemplated closing lines altogether, but ultimately concern about protests from local communities appears to have caused the railway to defer the plan. There were, however, some closures on Britain's railways during the period, with a fifth of the mileage being lost in Scotland. While most were branches, longer lines such as the Alnwick to Coldstream route were also axed.

In the period between the two world wars railways did begin (belatedly) to fight road competition: there was more use of motor vehicles, particularly to deliver goods and parcels from country stations, and in running their own bus services. Railways were slow to adopt diesel power, and only the Great Western made any real use of railcars, introducing a fleet of thirty-eight

Many railways introduced small, unstaffed halts to provide low-cost facilities in remoter locations. There was already a siding serving a local mill at Sarsden in rural Oxfordshire, and this halt was opened in 1906 to provide passenger facilities.

from 1934, a number of which were used on branches and less well-used cross-country lines. Steam still reigned supreme although government loans introduced after the Wall Street Crash enabled the Southern Railway to electrify a number of its branch lines in the south-east of England.

Just over twenty years after the end of the First World War, Britain found itself at war once again, and the question of how economic many country lines were was shelved for the duration. A number of branch lines serving coastal resorts were hard hit as holiday and excursion business disappeared almost overnight, but in the early part of the war railways in rural areas were also often the destinations for many of the thousands of evacuees moved by railway companies from large cities such as London, Birmingham, Bristol and Liverpool. The construction of hundreds of military depots and munitions facilities in country areas, most needing to be served by rail, meant that there were only a few line closures during the Second World War, with poorly used branches such as the Lybster & Wick Light Railway, the Weston, Clevedon & Portishead Railway and the Hay to Pontrilas line in Herefordshire amongst the casualties. While government discouraged all but essential passenger journeys by rail, goods traffic increased by 50 per cent as munitions, equipment and raw materials were transported around the country to support the war effort. In the run-up to D-Day in 1944 thousands of troops and the equipment required for the invasion were moved via cross-country routes to the south coast. The same railways also played a key role in handling ambulance trains once the invasion had begun, a role they had taken on in the First World War too.

After 1945 the railways were left to count the cost of the war, not only in terms of the men killed in the conflict, but also in the huge backlog of maintenance required to bring their operations back to anything like pre-war standards. Branch and minor lines had been particularly neglected, with old and worn-out locomotives and rolling stock remaining in use; following the nationalisation of the 'Big Four' companies in 1948 matters did not improve very quickly and the

The introduction of diesel railcars was seen as a way of cutting costs and making rural lines more economic, and their adoption was promoted by British Railways to both the public and staff.

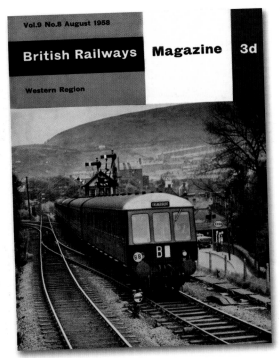

Vol.9 No.8 August 1958

British Railways Magazine 3d

Western Region

management of British Railways began shutting uneconomic branch lines in 1949 and 1950, well before the publication of the Beeching Report.

The publication of the long-awaited British Railways Modernisation Plan in 1954 made a number of important recommendations, not least that in order to survive BR needed to reduce its costs by closing uneconomic or duplicate lines. This meant that the pace of closures began to increase considerably, and the fact that well over 3,000 miles of line was closed between 1948 and 1962 suggests that the perception of all branch and minor line closures being attributable to Beeching is somewhat misleading. There were many well-known casualties during this era, including the Ashbourton to Totnes line (now the South Devon Railway), the Wye Valley branch, the Meon Valley line in Hampshire and the Peterborough to Yarmouth Beach line.

It was in the 1950s that the closures of branch or minor lines became more contentious. Although there had been closures in the past, the scale, speed and finality of the process struck a chord with local communities who rather belatedly realised they were losing a valuable amenity, even though it was not well used in many cases. There were many bitter and long-fought campaigns to keep lines open, with campaigners often complaining that BR

The sign of things to come: bus competition makes its presence felt on the West Somerset line.

End of an era: closing the crossing gates at Stanton on the Highworth branch line near Swindon. The line closed to passengers in 1953 although goods traffic and special trains for Swindon Works staff continued for another nine years.

had provided misleading and sometimes incorrect data about the financial performance of lines. The sad fact was that many branches had never made money, but their social value to a community was nevertheless high.

The Modernisation Plan also detailed the radical decision to replace steam locomotives on BR with diesel traction and to build a fleet of up to 4,600 railcars. The introduction of lightweight railcars had already begun in 1952 with some success in Yorkshire and a number of other locations, including branches on the Western Region. Further diesel multiple units were then built at Derby and Swindon and by private manufacturers such as Metro-Cammell and Cravens.

The cover of the Beeching Report.

BRITISH RAILWAYS BOARD

The Reshaping of British Railways

PART 1: REPORT

LONDON

HER MAJESTY'S STATIONERY OFFICE

The Modernisation Plan was not a success and losses continued to rise; British Railways made a loss of over £102 million in 1962 and, faced with this huge deficit, the government took more drastic action, appointing Dr Richard Beeching as Chairman of the British Railways Board. Within a year Beeching had produced his now infamous report, *The Reshaping of British Railways*, which was to have a profound effect on the remaining branch and minor cross-country railways in Britain. The report painted a depressing picture of a railway network that lost money on all operations except the movement of coal; most startling was Beeching's conclusion that stopping trains were by far the biggest loss maker. He noted that on an average branch line a £1 fare actually cost BR £5 through high operating costs, waste and low passenger numbers.

The outcome of the report was undoubtedly shocking for those who loved railways and for the local communities affected by closures. The Beeching Report led to more than 5,000 miles of line being axed and 2,363 stations being closed. In the twenty-five years between 1950 and 1975 the national rail network had been reduced from 21,000 route miles to 12,000 miles and the number of stations correspondingly reduced from over six thousand to around two thousand. As the 'Beeching Axe' fell, campaigners continued to fight closures, largely in vain, and, in scenes repeated all over the country, the last few days of service on branch or minor lines were normally celebrated by large numbers of enthusiasts descending on a line, taking a last trip and then marking the last day with what David St John Thomas called a 'branch line funeral'. Tickets were punched, a wreath placed on the smoke box of the locomotive and photographs were taken by railway enthusiasts and locals before the last train disappeared for good.

In some cases, lines remained open for some years for goods traffic, but most branches soon slipped into decay very quickly. Track was lifted, fixtures and fittings were removed from stations and land sold off. As the weeds and vegetation took over, there were some lines, however, that were revived,

A two-car British Railways Western Region Diesel Multiple Unit passes Coleford, the junction for the North Devon line on an Exeter to Plymouth service in October 1967.

as the fledgling railway preservation movement began to acquire branch lines from British Rail. Although most of the longer cross-country routes have not survived, some heritage railways have taken over sections of route: the Swindon & Cricklade now operates on part of the old MSWJR line, and the Gloucestershire & Warwickshire Railway on part of the route from Cheltenham to Honeybourne. Elsewhere, heritage railways thrive on old country lines. The Bluebell, East Sussex, Llangollen, Severn Valley, and Worth Valley railways are just some of those that now re-create something of the atmosphere of a rural railway in the heyday of steam. There are also numerous narrow-gauge lines, especially those in mid- and North Wales, where enthusiasts continue to operate railways.

While there are many miles of previously closed line now operated by heritage railways, thousands of miles of disused track still remain in the British countryside. Not all has returned to nature, or been purchased by farmers or landowners. The National Cycle Network is a 10,000-mile long network of old railway lines that has been developed by the environmental charity Sustrans and local authorities into a green resource used by cyclists and walkers. Many old country railways now have more people using them than they ever did in the age of steam, and along many of the routes much of the original infrastructure such as bridges, tunnels and buildings still survives.

Despite all the closures since the 1950s, the current national railway network still includes a number of surviving branch and cross-country lines away from the busy inter-city routes. Many branches remain popular routes for tourists and holidaymakers: in Cornwall trains still run on old GWR branch line routes to Falmouth and Looe in the south, to St Ives in the west and to Newquay on the north coast. In Hampshire the Lymington branch also survives, acting as a feeder for passengers wishing to travel across the Solent to the Isle of Wight. In the north of England, trains still run into the heart of the Lake District to Windermere while, on the east coast, trains still serve the fishing port of Whitby.

Cross-country routes in Wales and Scotland also continue to survive, remaining as a vital link for remote communities. In an era of continuing traffic congestion, and with rail travel continuing to grow, there are now plans to reopen and rebuild a number of lines axed in the Beeching era, including the cross-country 'Varsity Route' between Oxford and Cambridge and a number of long-closed branch lines. It seems that the country railway may once again be an important part of the nation's transport network, although in the twenty-first century they may look rather different from how they did when they were planned and built over a century and a half ago.

PLACES TO VISIT

There are over a hundred heritage railways and numerous steam centres and museums in Britain and Ireland. Details of these can be obtained from railway magazines and publications or via the Heritage Railways Association website: www.heritagerailways.com

The list reproduced here is by no means exhaustive, but amongst the railways and museums celebrating the age of the country line are:

The Bluebell Railway, Sheffield Park Station, East Sussex TN22 3QL.
  Telephone: 01825 720800.
  Website: www.bluebell-railway.co.uk

Buckinghamshire Railway Centre, Quainton Road Station, Quainton,
  near Aylesbury HP22 4BY.
  Telephone: 01296 655720.
  Website: www.bucksrailcentre.org

Didcot Railway Centre, Didcot, Oxfordshire OX11 5XP.
  Telephone: 01235 817200.
  Website: www.didcotrailwaycentre.org.uk

East Somerset Railway, Cranmore Railway Station, Cranmore,
  Shepton Mallet, Somerset BA4 4QP.
  Telephone: 01749 880417.
  Website: www.eastsomersetrailway.com

Isle of Wight Steam Railway, The Railway Station, Station Road, Havenstreet,
  Isle of Wight PO33 4DS.
  Telephone: 01983 882204.
  Website: www.iwsteamrailway.co.uk

Keighley & Worth Valley Railway, The Railway Station, Haworth, Keighley,
  West Yorkshire BD22 8NJ.
  Telephone: 01535 645214.
  Website: www.kwvr.co.uk

Kent & East Sussex Railway, Tenterden Town Station, Tenterden, Kent
  TN30 6HE.
  Telephone: 01580 765155.
  Website: www.kesr.org.uk

Llangollen Railway, The Station, Llangollen LL20 8SN.
  Telephone: 01978 860979.
  Website: www.llangollen-railway.co.uk

Opposite: The sight and sounds of GWR Steam Railmotor No. 93 on the Looe branch in 2012 recreated a scene not witnessed on a country railway for more than sixty years following the outstanding restoration of this forerunner to the diesel railcar.

National Railway Museum, Leeman Road, York YO26 6XJ.
Telephone: 01926 621261.
Website: www.nrm.org.uk

Nene Valley Railway, Wansford Station, Old Great North Road, Stibbington
PE8 6LR.
Telephone: 01780 784444.
Website: www.nvr.org.uk

North Norfolk Railway, Sheringham Station, Station Approach, Sheringham
NR26 8RA.
Telephone: 01263 820800.
Website: www.nnrailway.co.uk

North Yorkshire Moors Railway, 12 Park Street, Pickering, North Yorkshire
YO18 7AJ.
Telephone: 01751 473799.
Website: www.nymr.co.uk

Severn Valley Railway, The Railway Station, Bewdley, Worcestershire
DY12 1BG.
Telephone: 01299 403816.
Website: www.svr.co.uk

South Devon Railway, The Station, Dart Bridge Road, Buckfastleigh, Devon
TQ11 0DZ.
Telephone: 01364 644370 or 0843 357 1420.
Website: www.southdevonrailway.co.uk

Spa Valley Railway, West Station, Royal Tunbridge Wells, Kent TN2 5QY.
Telephone: 01892 537715.
Website: www.spavalleyrailway.co.uk

STEAM: Museum of the Great Western Railway, Kemble Drive, Swindon
SN2 2TA.
Telephone: 01793 466646.
Website: www.steam-museum.org.uk

Strathspey Railway, Aviemore Station, Aviemore PH22 1PY.
Telephone: 01479 810725.
Website: www.strathspeyrailway.co.uk

Swanage Railway, Station House, Swanage, Dorset BH19 1HB.
Telephone: 01929 425800.
Website: www.swanagerailway.co.uk

West Somerset Railway, Minehead Station, Warren Road, Minehead,
Somerset TA24 5BG.
Telephone: 01643 704996.
Website: www.west-somerset.co.uk

FURTHER READING

Atterbury, Paul. *Branch Line Britain*. David & Charles, 2006.

Atterbury, Paul. *Along Country Lines*. David & Charles, 2007.

Gwynne, Bob. *Railway Preservation in Britain*. Shire Publications, 2011.

Simmons, Jack. *The Railway in Town and Country, 1830–1914*. David & Charles, 1986.

Thomas, David St John. *The Country Railway*. Francis Lincoln, 2011.

Vaughan, John. *The Rise and Fall of British Railways: Branch and Minor Lines*. Haynes Publishing, 2011.

British Railways passenger enquiry staff at Aberystwyth station in a picture dating from the 1960s.

INDEX

Page numbers in italics refer to illustrations